Borrowed Coats

Other Books by Wilma Elizabeth McDaniel

Chapbooks:

The Wash Tub (Stories), Pioneer, 1976
Buttermilk Children, Stone Woman, 1976
With This Cracker Jack Ring, Stone Woman, 1977
Beneath the Water Tower, Stone Woman, 1978
The Fish Hook: Okie and Valley Prose and Poems, Seven Buffaloes, 1978
Shoes Without Laces and Other Hard Luck Poems, Stone Woman, 1979
A Homemade Dress, Stone Woman, 1979
Sand in My Bed, Stone Woman, 1980
Toll Bridge, Contact II, 1980
Who is San Andrea, Blue Cloud, 1984
Going Steady With R.C. Boley, M.A.F., 1984
The Manager of Sundown Hotel, Stone Woman, 1991
A River They Call Merced, Stone Woman, 1991
Hanging Out at the Avalon Café, Back Forty, 1996
We Live or Die in Pixley, Back Forty, 1999

Books:

The Red Coffee Can (Stories and Poems), Valley, 1974
Sister Vayda's Song, Hanging Loose, 1982
A Girl from Buttonwillow, Wormwood, 1990
A Primer for Buford, Hanging Loose, 1990
A Prince Albert Wind, Mother Road, 1994
The Last Dust Storm, Hanging Loose, 1995
The Ketchup Bottle, Chiron Review, 1996
Shirtwaist Women, Chiron Review, 1996
Weatherwatch, Back Forty, 1998
Wind Rocked Our Babies to Sleep, Mt. Aukum, 1999

Borrowed Coats

Wilma Elizabeth McDaniel

Hanging Loose Press
Brooklyn, New York

Copyright © 2001 by Wilma Elizabeth McDaniel

Published by Hanging Loose Press, 231 Wyckoff Street, Brooklyn, New York 11217-2208. All rights reserved. No part of this book may be reproduced without the publisher's written permission, except for brief quotations in reviews.

Printed in the United States of America
10 9 8 7 6 5 4 3 2 1

Some of these poems first appeared in the following magazines: *Free Lunch, Hanging Loose* and *South Valley Arts*.

Hanging Loose Press thanks the Literature Programs of the New York State Council on the Arts for grants in support of this book's publication.

Cover art and design by David Borchart
Cover photo of author by Kim Grossman

Library of Congress Cataloging-in-Publication Data

McDaniel, Wilma Elizabeth.
    Borrowed coats / Wilma Elizabeth McDaniel.
       p. cm.
    Poems.
    ISBN 1-882413-94-6 -- ISBN 1-882413-93-8 (pbk.)
      I. Title.
PS 3563.A272 B67 2001
811'.54--dc21   00-050037

Produced at The Print Center, Inc. 225 Varick St., New York, NY 10014, a non-profit facility for literary and arts-related publications. (212) 206-8465

Contents

Burned in the Test
Burned in the Test 11
A Zealot in Big Muddy 12
Could I Stop There 13
Can Crows Smell Jasmine 14
Frying Potatoes 15
Murder Past Midnight 16
Thoughts After Telephone Call 17
Waiting for a Train 18
My New Business 19
Finding Old Perfume Bottle 20
Entrapment 21
Going to Autographing in Foreign Car 22
New California Industry 23
Agreement 24
Suddenly I Remember 25
Breadstuff 26
Live and Let Live 27
January Reality, 1998 28
At Spring Yard Sale 29
We Never Called It Theatre 30
Where on Earth 31

Late Spring for a Catholic
Admission 35
My Question 36
To Boating Friends 37
In Their Company 38
In the Paradise Restaurant 39
Late Spring for a Catholic 40
Opal 41
The Extremist 42
Dignity 43
Some Day Soon 44
My Landlady Brings Me an Easter Gift 45
Sister Beuline's Advice 46

Surprise 47
Calling on a Bereaved Neighbor 48
I Never Felt Right. 49
Vigil with Aunt Maggie Bowman 50
Tonight Is Carnival. 51

Out of the Mouths
The Last Go-Around 55
A Grandfather's View 56
A Mother's Vocation. 57
My Brother and His Barber 58
I Have My Own Ideas 59
Mourners. 60
News on the Legal Front 61
Forty-Five-Year-Old Man on Total Disability. 62
Perfume Hound 63
Cornered 64
Reprimand at Rosewood Manor 65
Bonus Concert in Tulare, 1997 66
Friendship Fracture 67
A Proper Present 68
Revelation 69
A Blustery Palm Sunday in Tulare, California 70
Solution 71
I Would Like to Shoot the Quack 72
Is Woody Gilmore Only a Two-Timer 73
Maybe I Am All Wrong 74
Fastidious Leonard. 75
Bad Timing 76
After the Loss 77
Mismatch. 78
Out of the Mouths of Bail Bondsmen 79
Two Helens 80

Pies

Remembering	83
A Mug for Comfort	84
A Notable Death of 1949	85
California Frigid Zone, 1937	87
Literary Mentor	88
Let Yourself Go	89
Vineyard Phantasy	90
Nineteen Thirty	91
Courting Music	92
Inflation	93
Two Worlds	94
Opening My Mail	96
Obsession with Hunting Greens	97
A Fine Cuisine Memory	98
Ancestor	99
Sweat	100
Remembering Farm Women	101
Mrs. Percival's Toilet Water	102
Recollections of Homestead Uncle	103
Waiting Game, 1926	104
A Pagan Mystery	105
The Zane Grey Secret	106
Summer Hired Hand, 1926	107
Our Old Ways	108
Great Depression Tragedy	109
My Father's Brothers	110
Pies	111
Borrowed Coats	112

For my mother, Anna McDaniel

Burned in the Test

Burned in the Test

I have wasted so much
sunrise
scraping burned oatmeal
from a charred pot

I have often profaned
bright noon
into three pm
waiting by the telephone
for a call that never came

Why can't I be satisfied
to soak a pot overnight
and be content with new shoestrings
when the old ones snap

I have spent a cat's lifetime
tying short pieces together

I have glued broken handles
on many cups
waited days to find out
they never hold
and been burned in the test

A Zealot in Big Muddy

What did three quatrains and a couplet—
(Shakespearean or Petrarchan sonnets?)—
really mean to the seventh grade?

Miss Worley ranked them in importance
just below the Ten Commandments
She didn't use those exact words

but we saw that Sunday school gleam
in her Methodist eye

and when she stood before the class
with all the power of her ninety pounds
we could count the waves in her marcel

Could I Stop There

Today I changed from
plain graham crackers
to the new chocolate flavor

It made all the difference
and started me wondering if
I could wear eye shadow

Would it be like a blast
of chocolate
And could I stop there

Would I be a fool
with black smudges
under my astigmatic eyes

even go further astray
sampling Tahiti-red lipstick
at the cosmetic counter

and longing for
all the colors of Gauguin

Can Crows Smell Jasmine

Brother Crow
since you spend all
your daylight hours
parading through
my yard

May I politely ask
where do you live
when the sun goes down

What tree is your cottage
Who serves you supper

Is it the complaining one
who follows you all day

Does she change under a high moon
on swaying branches

Can crows smell jasmine
Do you kiss goodnight

Frying Potatoes

At one time
I would have tossed
this day off

as being dull
and not worth
fooling with

but that was before
Mrs Malvita Poston
moved here to Rosewood

with her style of cooking
and contempt of diets

Today she is frying potatoes—
already they are burning
which is part of the ritual

She will rush to the stove
and make a fuss
over stirring them
then put the lid back on
and walk away
until the potatoes reach
charred perfection

Murder Past Midnight

That cricket was unreasonable
I gave him every way out

I said "Look here—
you have messed up my sleep
for the past month

chirping under my bed
the second the light goes out
calling for your lady friend

Just vacate my apartment
go out the way you came in
(which is a mystery to me)
and I will forget your offense"

But he ignored me
and last night my heart was dark
even without a belligerent cricket
under my bed—
too many loves are going "there"

At 2 a.m. I got up with murder
in my heart
took a long-handled mop
and killed that scogger
after a twenty-minute fight

Thoughts After Telephone Call
December 28, 1996

You telephoned me from Buffalo
three days after Christmas

asked about my holidays
and the weather in California

I looked out the window
at a small lake

and started to complain
of excessive rain and cold

but you cut me off
with "California winters are nothing

You valley-ites never have
to shovel snow"

Of course you are correct
in that one sense

but you don't realize
how hard a California night can be in winter—

the leftover day must be dealt with
it can't be stored in the fridge

and the smell of disappointment lingers
longer than the salmon patties I fried tonight

Waiting for a Train

Two silly people
asked me point-blank

as if I were on trial
"How about romance?"

They didn't specify whose romance—
mine or the railroad's

and since I wasn't under oath
I didn't have to tell them

that this affair of the heart
has gone on for years

with midnight trains
writing me songs of love

which I always answer
from my darkened room

My New Business

You thought I had
retired from sweets

but no
here I go
to my candy shop

for now
I own this world
a business I've craved
all my life

I wear a white cap
to cover my hair
never pulled taffy tighter

I have mastered
peanut brittle
my lemon drops
won't sour your
mouth

my candy kisses
Hershey rich
are never too sweet
for one more kiss
my peppermint canes
will walk you home

Finding Old Perfume Bottle

This has gone
far enough—
stop the unpacking
I beg you

Put back the blue bottle
from down in the trunk
Can't you see yet

that "Evening in Paris"
was much better
in Kansas:

Great Bend
had dust storms
and great lovers
with grit in their teeth

Its women
were awesome—
they picked flowers
from high off the sun
to braid in their hair

I ask you again—
halt the unpacking
let love stay where it is
keep the cap on the bottle
slam the trunk lid hard

Entrapment

A patch on my heart
my face full of frowns
still you coaxed

"Do come with me
a couple hours
it will be fun
get you away from
your pain
and your prayers"

I only nodded
We went
too jauntily for me
to an oasis of plastic palms
and makeshift waterfalls

We entered through a door
stolen from a convent

Down the hall
I could hear steady buzzing
a hive of poets

Why didn't you warn me
that bees who tipple white wine
can be deadly

Going to Autographing in Foreign Car

I am uneasy in this car:
so small—where does the gas go?
So low
I fear the underside is dragging
on concrete
and worse than that
my new all-weather coat
must be swiping asphalt
from that stretch of Highway 43

and where Sir
will you park in Pygmyland
and who will stand by the door
to help you extract me
from this expensive
low-down toy

Well, keep driving to the signing
my boy—If I wanted to ride on a turtle
I would have stayed in Oklahoma
drifted down Big Muddy
with my feet dangling in the water
while willows brushed my hair
and the turtle never tired

New California Industry

I used to know exactly where I was
Now I must stand in the center
of the San Joaquin Valley
heart of my heart
to even locate where I belong

I look to the north—I see prisons
I scan the south—I see only prisons
where half a century ago wild flowers
spread a Persian carpet for guests

Now I pick my way through shattered lives
broken bottles
and half-buried guns and knives

I cannot forget
and do not allow myself to forget
that once I saw a giant condor
in the azure sky
and thought it was a mythical *roc*—

The only birds in these skies
are crime watch helicopters
swooping darkly above barred vans
seeking more desert land for prisons

Agreement
September 26, 1996

I look in my full-length mirror
from Ace Hardware—(six ninety-five
once in a lifetime price)
and agree with the mirror
that I am a beautiful woman
for the type I am

My hair is a haystack
my head classic pumpkin
smooth in the jaws
Halloween I don't fake—
these are my teeth

So many prizes go out
to cookie-cutter beauties
parading through life
what does that matter to me

I look in my mirror
thump on my head
agree again with the mirror
I am the best of my kind

Suddenly I Remember

Five years ago
American antiques
were all the rage

I hid Mama's oak rocker
from nosy dealers
also her pewter mugs

Now I can bring them out—
Asian art is definitely in
and Far East culture has hit our town

A local car dealer
placed a stone Buddha
in his backyard

a fry cook we know
has gone into debt for *Koi*
let his mortgage lapse

and two WASP neighbors
are studying Japanese
at the community college

Suddenly I remember
where I hid
Mama's rosewood Bible stand
safe to use again

Breadstuff

I have never liked bagels
even from Foxxy's in Las Vegas
where people thought
they were the best

I still don't like bagels
It is something
in my Okie culture
maybe in my genes

Breadstuff I do love
Pass the cornbread
toss me a biscuit
make me a flour tortilla

But please
don't lay any bagels on me
the way Good Life
forced them on derelicts
and women folding clothes
in the White Foam Laundromat

Live and Let Live

There was a stray dog
on my lawn tonight
apparently not a vicious animal
sneaking along behind me
in the sultry night

Sprinklers went on violently
and the dog lay down flat
on the wet grass
paws stretched out in
utter relief

I didn't have the heart
to call Animal Control
and leave a message
It is such a hard night—
why not live
and let live
as far as we poor ones can

Mother Teresa is dead
and Princess Diana
known in all the world
and I don't know the name
of that dog
though it must have been
something like "Tricky"

January Reality

The cost of living goes up
the perm in my hair
grows out
shall I try for waist-length
or make it to Paolo's?

He is Brasileiro
his hole-in-the-wall shop
so tiny
we must back in
only two chairs
(hard old-style)

and get a haircut and perm
for only ten dollars
Can you believe that?
It won't last long
He is too good
his eyes pure liquid

He will soon become
the trendy Paolo
and drop us ten-spot
ladies
for upscale women
who can pay sixty

Coda: It will happen.

At Spring Yard Sale

Without my consent
the cycle turns
sets the seasons:
peach-hot August
trails blackberry July

but already
this blowy April day
I am planning for winter

which doesn't seem right
with iris nodding around me
thin-veined and delicate:

There should be autumn asters
and thick-lashed daisies
strong and independent
not begging for anything

but with only
a dime's worth of time
what can I do
about the restless seasons

except buy this winter scene
painted on plyboard

We Never Called It Theatre

Live theater
actual faces with people's eyes
looking at us from the stage
various voices
old Ephraim in *Desire Under the Elms*

Sister and I had our favorites
in plays and playwrights
That funny wicked Noel Coward
with *Hay Fever*
the woman who played Sorel Bliss
was bliss itself

We wished our brothers H and K
could have been with us
at *Shenandoah*
but they were farther away
than just across the wide Missouri

Where on Earth

August 24, 1980

Not everyone in his family had died, but there were only four siblings left the morning Sheldon Rising came, with tomatoes from his garden that were even more beautiful than the ones he'd brought us the summer before. We invited him in for coffee but he told us he couldn't stay, stood there at the door for just a minute. Such a frail, gentle man, with amazing blue eyes. Then he drove off in his old pickup. I went straight to the kitchen and ate two big tomatoes, standing over the sink. It was heaven, with the red juice squirting around my mouth. A few drops fell on my dress with its speckled bird's-egg print. Where on earth did I get such material for a dress? It must have been that hole-in-the-wall yardage shop that closed after three weeks.

*Late Spring
for a Catholic*

Admission

I worry too much
about heavy stuff:
That I realize—

So foolish of me
for this and that

things above
my simple mind

when I don't even know
how I got here

All directions are blanks to me
road maps a migraine headache

Why can't I reason
with myself?

Why should I worry
just because I don't
know the way
out of this place either?

My Question

Why don't bells toll

My brother's heart broke
in four pieces
and he is dead in El Paso

The rest of the town mourns:
the Rio Grande's gone dry
gamecocks won't fight
red chilis don't burn

rattlesnakes defanged
scorpions retired

police are in a coma
Larry McMurtry's left Texas

So why don't bells toll
from the poor stucco church

where Brother prayed by the hour
and his tears flooded the pews

To Boating Friends

Even if I threw
my life overboard
with the likes of you
and came up choking
in the midst
of seaweed
and starfish
my eyes would be
in the back of my head
looking for dry land
dusty cracked earth
bird tracks
snake prints
crossing my homeward path—
I would be calling for them
even if I were going down
for the third time.

In Their Company

I really am patient
most of the time

but there is a limit
to this waiting around

for a glimpse of my gang
who lit out
for greener pastures

Not that I begrudge them
a better deal
I just long to be
in their scruffy company again

even if they have tidied up their acts
become boring little saints

In the Paradise Restaurant

My first visit here
Across the room
I see a woman in rose

I hear her laughter
at a remark
not meant for me
a stranger in Paradise

She repeats the remark
"A Catholic in Oklahoma
is that such a big deal?"

I stir rice on my plate
and mouth words
silently
to the woman in rose
so little she knows

A Catholic in Oklahoma
a snowball in hell
How long did they last?
Which ones melted and ran
when the fire burned hot?

then I asked the waitress
to bring more tea

Late Spring for a Catholic

It is a cold day for spring
bluish and keep-your-distance
an impossible time for a fling
with the Sierra Nevada

I have no snowshoes
and would die at high altitude
so I am saved from excess
and turn up the heat

Shall I brew my best tea
or save it for the visitors:
a girl with gray eyes
a man with bad scars

or shall I open the old book
where a purple ribbon marks Lent

Opal

September 30, 1995

Sister finally got
a storm named after her
How fitting
I bet the winds are
angry
auburn color
and they
have their say
however long
it takes
to blow anger
out to sea

The Extremist

I may be something
of a nitpicker
but I hope not a nitwit

I do rail
whenever I see
a TV preacher driving
a Dusenberg

I grab a mop
and beat the life
out of helpless spiders

I may be a bit extreme
but let the high roller preachers
stay away from Cannes
and drive economy cars
use their gas in the pulpit
high octane for the Lord

I could go for that
write a small check
even sign it

Dignity

I smooth my sheets
plump the pillows
spread a patchwork quilt
and hide my nightgown
in the closet

God grant one favor:
that no paramedic
will ever find me in it
dead
and gone where I am going

May the gown hang in dignity
unseen
May I depart in sweats
and heavy shoes
Selected Poems of Thomas McGrath
under my left arm
a magnifying glass in my purse

Some Day Soon

Telephone poles are holy—
Look
how they form a line
of Latin crosses

all the way from Tipton
to Pixley
the smell of dairy growing stronger
by the mile

How devout Portuguese milkers
really are:
They cross themselves
dozens of times each day
and never even know it
as they pass beneath the poles

Their indulgences are piling up
and some day
will reach to Heaven—
a special corner
smelling of Grade A milk

My Landlady Brings Me an Easter Gift

She brought me a pot
of African violets
deepest purple

fleshiest blossoms
that ever grew
in Kmart's garden

and she laughed
with a bell in her voice

that rang all the way
to Tipton on the south

flung her hair about
in that sunlit shade
of a blonde woman
turned fifty
living like thirty
and getting away with it

having no doubt
she will retain that laugh
and shade of hair till ninety

Sister Beuline's Advice

After that last red-hot revival, when the evangelist claimed to have seen several of his flock in Hell's flames, his sermon got to Sister Beuline. She even tore up her recipé for devil's food cake and urged my mother to do the same. She said a cake named for the devil didn't have any place on a saved woman's table. Mama just gave her a kind look and ordered more chocolate from the Rawleigh man.

Surprise

Nora is a pious girl
She has every right
to be fundamental
as they come

Mitch likes to tease her
I heard him ask
"Do you really believe
in angels?
Have you seen one today?"

That was when he and I
got a big surprise
Nora hit him across the mouth
so hard his lips began
to swell bluish
and she gathered up
her Bible and walked off

Calling on a Bereaved Neighbor

Esther is a hard woman
to love
and she never liked me

I had to whip myself
to her house
when I heard the news

She met me at the door
her eyes cold dry
and said "I'm glad you came"

and took me to the kitchen
where she was making
a casserole

"Why don't men take care of
themselves"
she complained matter-of-factly

"It was like John wanted to die
and get away from me—
lifting those wheelbarrows of

rocks he didn't need for any reason
just something to keep him
in motion"

I Never Felt Right

Aunt Rose made coffee
for the two of us
while we waited for
the coroner's release

"You must never again"
she told me severely
"let death find you
without a black dress

"I never felt right
going to Jack's funeral
in a pink dress
the only one I had

"There I was
among his womenfolks
in their grieving black dresses"

The sadness in her voice
sounded as if Uncle Jack
had died last year
instead of 1940

Vigil with Aunt Maggie Bowman

Darman phoned me
from a garage
a lump of dread choking
his voice

"You better go," he said
"There isn't much time
and you know her
old ways better than I"

which is true
though Aunt Maggie
probably doesn't know
I am here

Her body feels cool
as the sheets
but she must be burning
inside her memory

"The old well"
she keeps saying
"Draw a fresh bucket
and give me a drink"
She stirs on the pillow
"and tie up the morning glories"

Tonight Is Carnival

Under the lamp
with the shade that turns yellow
when the light comes on

I drink tea with a scholar
who swept in smiling
a Russian translation in her bag

carrying every good thing for me:
lace cookies and ice cream
a loaf of dark bread and two stories
from North Beach

At that point I told the stories
I'd overheard in Farmersville
better than anything from San Francisco

The scholar checked the calendar
said Lent was coming right up—
how it all fits together

Tonight is carnival in Tulare
a three-ring circus
a triple-decker ice cream cone
strands of beads thrown from a float

Out of the Mouths

The Last Go-Around

Cletus looks good for sixty
and the hard traveling
he has done. A girl at the
beauty shop confessed she
keeps his bronze hair all
one color.

I saw him recently down
at the Korner Kitchen. He
had a three-stack before him
and was slathering on soft
margarine and maple syrup
and talking to the regulars who
eat breakfast there.

"Yeah, you heard it right.
I'm gonna tie the knot again.
You don't know her, a little
redhead from Yuba City.
How many times does
this make?"

He put down his fork and
counted on his left hand.
"Marge, Mary, Lavelle, and Betty.
That makes four, don't it?
Well I can tell you for certain
this is my last go-around."

A Grandfather's View

Mister Marshall takes
A dim view
Of modern music

"Why the names alone
are enough
to corrupt youth

"*Sting*
Red Hot
The Grateful Dead
Their leader died—
Whether he was grateful or not
the old boy passed on

"And this new one
My grandkids are raving about
Big House

"Don't that remind you
Of a penitentiary?
Like 'going up the river'
When we meant
Sing Sing"

A Mother's Vocation

I don't know how
God feels
about the subject

but little Andy's mother
has already
called him
to a priestly vocation

I remember
when he was
only four
she made him
a monk's habit
from an old bathrobe

and tied it
around his waist
with drapery cord

She was so proud
"Look at him
A perfect little
Thomas Merton
Anyone can see it"

My Brother and His Barber

My fussy silver-haired brother
came home neatly trimmed

and told me while
taking down a coffee mug

"My barber makes me nervous
the man unloads
his entire life on me
with every haircut

"He tells me about his bills
the dirty deals
his various wives pulled on him

"child support for kids
who never send him
a birthday card

"He leaves nothing out
takes more time
than I have hair
just to finish his story

"He does know how
to cut my hair
but I would quit him in a heartbeat
if I could find
another barber
half as good"

I Have My Own Ideas

I know for a fact
she is an MD
fully licensed
and has a practice
in LA

But why does she spend
every weekend
at rodeos here in the
dusty San Joaquin Valley
wearing jeans and cowboy boots

trying to get acquainted
with every cowboy
and bull rider
on the Western circuit

talking like a girl
who wouldn't know
a stethoscope
if she saw one

I have my own ideas
about this situation
from her end of a conversation
I overheard
at the pay phone

Mourners

Bob and Wendy drove up
from Glendale and spent
last night with me

I don't think they slept at all
These apartment walls are thin and
each time I awoke
I could hear them talking low

They are taking Jerry Garcia's
death very hard
and that won't help Bob's
irregular heartbeat

I set the coffee maker
for them and put out
cinnamon rolls to heat
dozed off and didn't awaken
until six-thirty

They had drunk half a pot
of coffee
then left for the Bay area
and Jerry's funeral

News on the Legal Front

Twenty-one trees
the lawyers planted
on Volunteer Saturday

strange sight indeed
sweating dungarees
twenty-one redwoods

soquels and Aptos blue
grow five feet a year
and last five thousand years

twenty-one trees
all donated eagerly
by Valley nurseries

Nary a lawyer
struck a deal or
billed a client

while mockingbirds
surveyed the scene
and serenaded all

Forty-Five-Year-Old Man
On Total Disability

Some of the bored and
nosy tenants
at Golden Age Gardens
challenged the newcomer

"Man, you're too young
to be living in this place
How did you pull it off"

and they crowded around
and wondered about
his wide belt
with a Zuni silver buckle
and asked if he shouldn't
have to sell it
to offset his low rent

at that point
Maggie Case spoke up
"You fools
don't have enough brains
among you
to fill a bird's skull

"What do want to see?
This man thrown out
on the street
because he has a nice
belt buckle? Get real!"

Perfume Hound

Here in Oleander Gardens
where men are only
three percent
women hide at the sight of one man

who always asks
if he gets near enough
"what scent is that

"*White Shoulders*
Tabu
or maybe *Opium*?"

I heard a widow of ninety-two
yell back at him
"This is Avon's *August Roses*"
then she hobbled away
as fast as a metal walker can

and left him sniffing the air
trying to remember all
the fragrances
women wear

Cornered

I knew Herb's crafty eyes
were on the vacant seat
of the county Board of Supervisors
when he came and started to
talk to our group at Rosewood

trying his best to be so erudite
and not fooling anyone
except the tenant in number 17
whose eyes never left Herb
when he cleared his throat
and announced

"Ladies and gentlemen
we have almost reached the end
of two millennia
and we can expect changes of
enormous consequence"

The tenant from number 17
raised a bony hand
and asked earnestly
"What kind of changes will there be?
Do you think we will get lower
rent and better treatment?"

He was so innocent in his question
that Herb was thrown for a loss
couldn't reconnect with the high flying
words of his election pitch
they just floated away from him

He looked at the refreshment table
and said with relief
"Let's knock off and have some of
the goodies over there"

Reprimand at Rosewood Manor
July 2, 1995

The old rooster forgets
his true age
and struts
even though his spurs
are blunted
his crown drooping
He crows
a bawdy mouthful

The manager takes him
aside firmly and reminds him
"this is a mixed crowd
see those women
go get
yourself a glass
of punch
and sit down
Please"

Bonus Concert in Tulare, 1997

"You don't really believe
Wynona will open the fair
here tomorrow?"

"She certainly will
You *must* hear her
All you need do
is whip on down here
from Goshen

"Ruthie
don't you understand
it wouldn't cost you
a cotton-picking penny
to hear Wynona
through my screen door

"Better still
we can sit outside
to catch a breeze
and Wynona's voice
will come over nice
and clear

"Just the way it did
for Reba McIntyre
and Randy Travis"

Friendship Fracture

"Yes we had been friends
for many years
but that's over
since Merle Haggard came to town"

Joanne said "Bea
could have told me
tickets were going on sale
at the fair grounds
saved me a place in line
called me on that phone
she always carries

"I'd have raced across town
red light or high water
speeding ticket
or rowboat
nothing at all

"But no
she didn't even tell me
she'd got tickets
for all her family
until the show was over
like she didn't want me
to hear Merle
I can't figure it any other way"

A Proper Present

Aunt Boots' children
knew her birth date
marked it red
on the calendar

but they had no idea
what present to give
on her ninetieth birthday

One son suggested
a cruise to the Bahamas
while it was winter
in Nebraska

A daughter reminded him
"Mama gets seasick looking at a full bathtub"

A great-grandson
and eight-year-old
country music freak
piped up
"I know what Grammy
would like better than
anything—
that new album to Jimmie Rodgers"

His father said in wonderment
"What a coup
Grandma had all Jimmie's original
records when we were kids
Don't know what happened to them"

Revelation

When three of us
were eating in Molly's Café
Herlan volunteered
(certainly no one asked him):

"Do you know I was an orphan
Someone left me in front
of Good Hope House

"without even a note
pinned to my blanket—
the nurses judged me
to be about one month old

"I grew
but I never was your
Ivory Soap baby—
No one wanted to adopt
a flat-faced kid
with red straw for hair

"I stayed in the orphanage
until FDR wanted me
for the CCC
and paid me a dollar a day
for doing work I loved"

A Blustery Palm Sunday in Tulare, California 4-9-95

Wind is howling
sand is stinging our town's face
palms are waving in Jerusalem
and palms are waving here
at every tumbleweed

Women are previewing
their Easter finery
one week early—
I saw a yellow hat
come out of brunch
at Apple Annie's
and blow away forever

Outside Long John Silver's
the wind whipped off
a man's toupee—
the lady with him
was quite upset
and wouldn't get in the car

Solution

I knew Neva's Pentecostal parents
opposed the engagement because
her fiancé had not been saved

and made it clear to them
he had no desire to be saved
which caused them to predict
disaster for their daughter

Yet Neva with the mousy hair
learned to make
her marriage work
(as she related to me looking back)

When Clete shaved he cussed the world
and everyone in it
somehow it helped him start his day
but it shocked the life out of her

She started taking her coffee outside
and listening to the birds for half an hour
When she returned to the house
Clete was cleanshaven and happy
and ready for two hard-fried eggs

"It wasn't really hard" Neva explained
"once I learned how to handle him"

I Would Like to Shoot the Quack

Our neighbor Vance turned bitter
in his last years
and vented his feelings
on anyone within hearing

"Don't give up anything you crave"
he ranted
"like coffee—
if you love the stuff
the way I do
keep a pot going all the time
bacon and eggs
eat 'em every day you live

"I would still like to shoot the quack
who convinced my wife
that this combination
would clog arteries and lead
to an early death

"I didn't really have to shoot him
He keeled over with a heart attack
clogged arteries at fifty-three
too much oat bran and broccoli

"How I miss all the good stuff
I could have had those long years:
I hope that quack spends Purgatory
in pork rinds"

Is Woody Gilmore a Two-Timer

I came home really bamboozled today. I don't know what to make of this situation. I saw Ruby hanging out at the Durango Café with Woody Gilmore. I don't believe everything I hear but I was quite jarred. I've known Ruby a long time. She swore to me that she was through with Woody forever.

They never saw me in a back booth. I could hear them ordering *chili verde* just like old times, and Mexican beer, and Woody even improvised on a Patsy Cline song: "I've got your picture and he's got you."

They laughed and pretty soon they called the waitress to bring more *cerveza* and I kept remembering how Ruby looked when she heard Woody had gone back to his wife after being separated for years and she said she didn't want to see that two-timer any nearer to Hanford than Mobile, Alabama.

Yeah, I've heard that song before. What could have changed? Has Woody's wife died, or is he just what Ruby called him, a two-timer?

Maybe I Am All Wrong

She is a second cousin
from Kokomo
a nice square lady
a prize jelly maker

She phoned me worried:
"Is there such a place
as the Crystal Palace in
Bakersfield

"From what I've heard
it doesn't fit the picture
of pumping oil wells
and blowing tumbleweeds

"But my grandson Clay swears
it's a landmark bar and theatre
Buck Owens built around his
1971 Pontiac Granville

"That doesn't mean boo to me
but maybe I am all wrong
Is there such a place?

"We are coming to California
on a trip in April
and Clay is my driver"

She laughed a little
"and in my car
using my credit card"

Fastidious Leonard

A newspaper plops
on the walk
coffee perks
and the moon is still up
when Leonard shaves:

the only sanitation employee
who smells of *Musk*
at six a.m.

and doesn't mind
his fellow workers
who joke
"Leonard is the only man
who can fall into
a garbage dump

and come up smelling
like a rose"

Bad Timing

We love Clifford alright, but we were sorry that he showed up when our cousin Nora was visiting. We knew his arrival meant only one thing. He brought all his George Bush paraphernalia with him, buttons, stickers, flyers, in a large old briefcase. I knew that was a mistake. He should have left that stuff in his van along with the giant Goldwater placards he still saves. Clifford has no discretion.

Right off, sparks began to fly from Nora—she came right to the point and said "I would like to see every Bush-ite carried out of town on a rail. They are a rich heartless group."

It was becoming very awkward in the living room. As hostess, I said, "let us have some dessert. Who wants regular coffee and who wants decaf?"

After the Loss

I think Mona is coming to life again, thank heaven. She said her son Nick wants to be the Lion King this Halloween and Bobby wants to go as Spiderman, but she can't find those costumes here and must go all the way to Bakersfield where they have a huge Halloween display at Party Works—dozens of characters. Mona said her boys asked, "Mama, why don't you dress up like Cinderella and go around with us trick or treating?" And Mona told them, "I might just do that very thing."

Mismatch

I always liked Guy
and I still think the boy
could have done better

He is from a poor background
and strangely awed
by Marlene's father
a pencil-necked CPA
who keeps a family crest
above his office desk

Guy drives a sanitation truck
has never missed a day
can retire in twenty years with a pension

The in-laws do admire Guy's
wonderful good looks
and Marlene's crowd cannot believe
such a hunk would fall to her

I heard a sharp-eyed woman
at the Sunday smorgasbord saying
after Marlene and Guy had passed
"If that princely man
ever learns basic grammar
Marlene will be back
where he found her"

Out of the Mouths of Bail Bondsmen

Little Joey arrived late
in life after Herman and Beth
had given up on having
a baby of their own

Joey is very bright
and picks up things fast
from the neighborhood kids
mostly Mexican
and Filipino children

Beth heard him using
a totally new word
It sounded like *encarcelado*
She had her neighbor Lupe
interpret for her

"Why it means someone in jail
You see it a lot in bail bonds"
and she showed Beth eight
such ads in the telephone directory
some with tricky slogans

If you don't like it behind the wall
give Speedy McFerrin a call

Two Helens

As our school principal escorted him out to the bleachers for the big game, I overheard the visiting professor say he taught Greek at Berkeley.

The professor didn't look much like a sports enthusiast. He was scrawny, with a bread dough personality. But I have to say he had a quick eye for the girls.

About that time our number one cheerleader Helen Boles led her pom-pom girls out on the field. She was a raven-haired beauty, easily the most gorgeous girl at LHS.

The principal said "Here comes Helen, our own homecoming queen." The doughy professor straightened up and said with real conviction, "Helen of Troy never looked this good."

The principal was pleased and said modestly, "Helen of Troy might have launched a thousand ships, but she couldn't have inspired the *Gauchos* the way our Helen has."

Pies

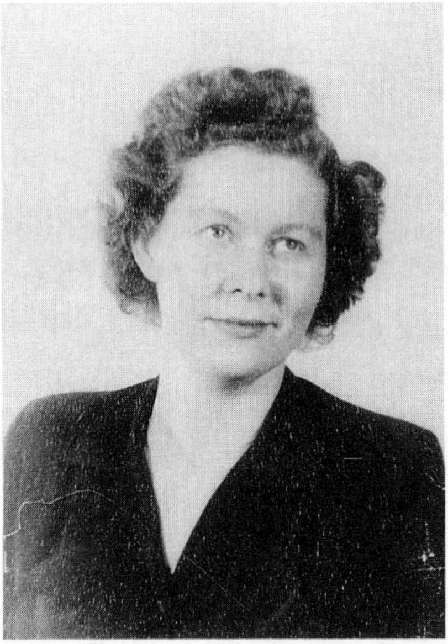

Remembering

I don't know why
I wrote so much
when I was twenty-seven

and let that woman
cut my hair
and listened
when she demanded
"take off your glasses
for this shot

"We already know
you write poetry
and it wouldn't hurt you
to wear a little lipstick"

A Mug for Comfort

This sturdy gray mug
stood out:
a motel maid
among fragile fine ladies
in the china shop

a stepchild really
and not blood kin—
for that reason I chose her

She has comforted me
many mornings
when the sun refused to rise

In appreciation
I have put a silver spoon
in her mouth
solid silver circa 1819
from Great-Grandpa's knapsack

A Notable Death of 1949

As yet the sky
had not caved in
our old fig tree
gave us fat fruit
and we were happy

until we turned on
the radio at noon
and heard
 "Leadbelly is dead
from Lou Gehrig's disease"

Then we fell apart
became basket cases
Rory took the news
even harder than I
at least outwardly

He walked through the house
singing snatches of
*Let the Midnight Special
Shine Her Light on Me*

His voice cracked
and he broke down
when he tried
Take This Hammer

I needed to be alone
and went out on the porch
all I wanted to sing was
Goodnight Irene

but it was broad daylight
on North F Street
a Pepsi truck rumbled past
and Mama's petunias were stirring
in the breeze

California Frigid Zone 1937

It should not have been
so hard to understand

a peach
a smile
a yellow pencil
I only wanted something
warm

but California showed me
an icy face each morning
gave me cold shoulder
every night

A vandal
it threw out my poems
from a shoe box

while I picked grapes
and wrote more verses
in the sand

Who knows why
I could not erase a word
blot out a single tear—
nor did I try to
that lifelong year

Literary Mentor

Cousin Truman
had finished one year at Tulsa U
when he came to California
on a working vacation

To tell the truth
he picked very few grapes
That part didn't matter:

He filled the hours
between hot sandy rows
with stories
that lit my teen-age mind

"Saint X"
he declared one day
"What a writer
what a life he led
flying the mail between
Dakar and Algiers
in those flimsy crates"
and he quoted from
Wind Sand and Stars

Remembering the book
he had become emotionally lost
in the Sahara Desert
and told me dreamily

"Cousin you're a girl
but you have to read this stuff
for yourself
try to broaden your mind"

Let Yourself Go

Corrina hated picking grapes
and tying up their vines

but there was no other way
to mine silver from sand

dimes quarters half-dollars
never silver dollar bonanzas

to stash away in a cup
with no handle

Corrina wanted to dance
Fred Astaire-Ginger Rogers style

When you hear that
hot marimba
loosen up and hit the timber
let yourself go

She found an old pair
of tap shoes at Goodwill
and wore holes in
Aunt Eulia's Congoleum rug

we could hear her tapping
out of the house
down the road forever
toward San Francisco

Vineyard Phantasy

I felt sorry for the boy
He was alone
and boarded somewhere

and used to pick grapes
with us
at old man Peroni's vineyard

He didn't mix much
with other workers
He would sing all day—one song:

"Some day
you're gonna miss me baby
some day
you're gonna feel so lonely"

Buster took him a drink of water
and the boy said
his name was Morgan

and he sang that song
because he wanted
to think a girl had thrown him out
when to tell the truth
he never had a girl to start with

1930-31

This faded yellow snapshot unsettles my memory of my departed oldest brother. He and his long tall pal Smokey Fiscus were working in the grapes at Arvin, 1930-31. They would work until the harvest was over and save whatever money they could. Before the fog settled over the valley they would go to Los Angeles and rent a cheap clean place from a widow with canaries. It was warm there and the air pure and since employment was scarce they had plenty of time to explore the area. Vernon would laugh and say, "When things got a little dull we could always go to Angelus Temple and see Sister Aimee Semple McPherson. It was the best show in town and free."

Courting Music

Cousin Mick was my favorite
a good sharing Okie boy
I remember he saved his peach picking
money and bought a battery-operated
radio from Monkey Ward

Through his open door we could hear
Little Richard
and Fats Domino—
Jerry Lee Lewis
nearly drove Uncle Doc crazy

About that time we began to hear
Les Paul and Mary Ford
How High the Moon
Blue Skies
Caravan

then one evening we heard
"Take my hand
and we're halfway there"

This last song caused Uncle Doc
to get a faraway look in his eyes
"Now that's what I call
courting music" he said

went to his bedroom
and brought Aunt Stacey's old fringed shawl
laid it across the back of his recliner
and sat down with his head against it

Inflation

Vonda must have been
the best-looking girl in
Merced County in the 1930s
and still looked good widowed
when she came to visit
from Houston this spring

I was surprised at her interest
in the place
she asked if the Fruit Basket in
Madera was still operating off
old Highway 99

She remembered
stopping there in 1936
with Cliff, the man she married later
She said they had pie and coffee
and the bill was only thirty cents

She remembered nice size pieces
of pie and real coffee
and there were tears in her violet eyes

It reminded me of the way she
looked when Cliff was knocked
cold in a football game with Turlock

Two Worlds

Ervin Pike
was what girls called
a sweet boy
safe to walk home with

His hair curled white-trash long
around his neck
before it became high style
He was too poor for a barber
and hated home crock cuts

the last time I saw Ervin in Oklahoma
was in front of Big Muddy Mercantile
He said his father was about
ready to give up farming
and head for California

The next time I saw him
was on Main Street in Merced 1937
in front of the Merced Theater
I didn't recognize him at first glance
hair cut short—still shiny, thick—
he had given up bib overalls
for black dress pants and a silky shirt

There was a girl with him
slim as a reed
with the blondest hair
I ever saw
so pretty she hurt my eyes

I never let on to little Buster
that I saw Ervin ahead of us
We got our tickets

and sat several rows back of them
Once there was a space between
patrons' heads
and I saw Ervin kiss the girl

Opening My Mail

He wrote me in a jerky hand
in care of the postmaster
no street address
no house number
just *Poet*
and my hometown

"My life is unsettled
nothing in the right place"
he wrote on yellow paper

"I didn't know where to start
but after I read that one book
of yours
I know I have to find myself
a battered old Stetson
with my grandfather's history

"I don't smoke Prince Albert
but now when I smell it
drifting down the streets
I know my ancestors are seeking me
and I am half-crazy to meet them"

Obsession with Hunting Greens

Orville is a tax consultant
and good at it
a rather cold-eyed type
but if you ever get to know him
I mean really know him
out on a golf course
on the manicured links
at some point he will break down
and talk about picking greens
with his mother
back in the bottomlands of Arkansas
He will lean on a club and tell you solemnly

"I carried a tin dishpan for Mama
and followed behind her
When she spotted the best greens
she would stoop down and cut them
with a sharp little knife
I remember dandelion and dock
wild lettuce and pokeroot"
He will frown when he mentions pokeroot

"The berries made beautiful purple ink
but they were poisonous and I'm not sure
the roots weren't
but Mama cooked them down with
salt pork and we never had any trouble"

A Fine Cuisine Memory

It now seems incredible
to me that once I knew
three Kickapoo indians
in Oklahoma
who opened a Mexican café
and called it El Burrito
and kept burros in a pen
just outside of town

These boys had no experience
with Mexican cuisine
but they hired Tico Chavez
as chef and cleanup man
after he hurt his back
and couldn't lift feed sacks
at the mill

Tico's wife Rosie helped him on weekends
always took the customers' money
because Tico couldn't make change

Papa loved Tico's chili
would make his own change
on weekdays if he came to town
told me before he died
"That boy Tico made real chili"

Ancestor

A God-fearing man
with a buggy whip
was hard to live with

Hard on his children:
strapping boys
with rebellious eyes
frail girls
in the shade of bonnets

King Cotton
and the buggy whip
ruled them all

and it was even hard
on God
having to listen to his
own words
read devoutly every night

by a man with a buggy whip
hanging on the wall behind
his chair

Sweat

When I was spindly four, when the world was all Easter egg colored, good folks read from the Bible every day Some could quote the preacher's words before he got them out. Some of the words stayed with me, the part where God told Adam to earn his bread by the sweat of his brow. That was hard. On a hot June day I felt my forehead to see if it was wet, then I buttered a high golden biscuit.

When Papa passed the plate around, I saw his sleeves were wet in the armpits. He told Uncle Prez, "I'm sure glad to finish off that north field before noon. It's a real scorcher."

I ate my biscuit while the butter was melting, and thought about the Bible. Maybe Papa and Uncle were earning their bread by the sweat of their brow and under their arms. I wondered if Mama earned her bread by baking it.

Remembering Farm Women

As a child
I watched them
and I remember

a woman's defense
was anything in reach

Her weapons were few
and always begrudged

Why did men imagine
they deserved the velvet touch
the nightingale's voice

from a woman who plowed
when planting got behind

and prayed for rainwater
to wash her hair

Why did rough farmers
dream of girls
from the Ziegfeld Follies

when wives were vomiting
with another pregnancy

Mrs Percival's Toilet Water

I knew her smell
through seven years
from five to twelve

For me
blue lilac toilet water
meant Mrs Percival

I had seen the bottle
on her dressing table
and wondered why
she didn't use rose water

Too young to know
women are as different
as the scents they choose
to wear
or in some cases
not wear

Preacher Philpot's wife
said perfume was a snare
of Satan

though she loved her own
flower garden
sat swinging on her porch
breathing its heavy fragrance

Recollections of Homestead Uncle

"It was hard
out there in early day
New Mexico

If someone got bad sick
we used Indian herbs
or poultices on them

If they were really strong
they would pull through
and thank God

Looking back
I never met an atheist
homesteader

For sure there were none
When the Reaper came
they bowed to him

and prayed there wouldn't
be a bad sandstorm
until we closed the grave
and piled rocks on it
to keep the sand
from blowing away"

Waiting Game, 1926

Ground was sandy cool and easy
I saw Jack Pelton
dig a hole
beneath the cottonwood
and bury a fruit jar
of moonshine whiskey

He patted the mound
smoothed it off
and disappeared
into the blackjacks

I could have told someone
Papa or Uncle Prez
but I wanted to have
one secret to myself

Perhaps if I waited
long enough
I would see Jack dig
the jar up

Men said whiskey
had to age
How long would it take
Would I be old enough to vote
or go with boys to the pie supper
whichever came first

Coda: True, about the whiskey, I saw it.

A Pagan Mystery

I had many country cousins
Among them was Mobley
He lived in Tulsa
and wore cologne
said it was aftershave

I was only eight
but I remember he went crazy
the first time he heard
"The Pagan Love Song"

He bought the record
and played it on the Victrola
over and over

Cousin Nona May
said she wasn't surprised
at Mobley's choice—
He had always been
a pagan

I didn't know what to make
of her indictment
Mobley taught Sunday School
and gave his testimony
at every prayer meeting

The Zane Grey Secret

Papa called Rory several times
really loud "Go find that stray calf"
He could have been heard as far away
as Gypsy Corner
but Rory never answered
He couldn't be found
for a very good reason
He was down by the pond
in the mulberry grove
smoking long lengths of
dry grapevines
and reading *Under the Tonto Rim*

At suppertime his lips were
purplish blue
but I didn't tell on him
I wanted to read that book
after he finished
I was only eight and a half
but I could read as well as
he could at eleven
He borrowed books from
Mister Rowan
who had a complete collection
of Zane Grey novels
and loaned them to a few worthy readers

Summer Hired Hand, 1926

He came from Osage County
I remember he had warm brown eyes
and was from a hard motherless family
Somehow he turned out gentle and
wise for fifteen and worked like a beaver

Mama took him in like a son
asked about his eating habits
what he liked and didn't like

"About breakfast" he answered politely
"Don't give me no shredded wheat
or puffed rice
That is food for city folks
Just fry me two eggs over once
and give me a few biscuits

"I am real easy to please
Just don't shake me out no
haystack cereal from a box"

Our Old Ways

The most charming man
I ever met
had seven producing oil wells
and crumbled crackers in his chili
He didn't realize he had become
very wealthy

still ate at Poor Boy's Cafe
instead of floorboarding
his gleaming Packard to Tulsa's
steakhouses

I had to take a message
to Mattie the cook at Poor Boy's
and found Mister Compton
having a late bowl of chili

I had grown since he saw me
but he said "you're Ben's daughter"
and called, "Mattie, cut Miss Wilma
a piece of lemon pie"

Steeped in Mama's counsel, I hung back
but Mr Compton assured me "Honey
I know your daddy and our old ways
You can eat with me"
and I sat down on the stool beside him

Great Depression Tragedy

Kinfolk edged closer
around the potbelly stove
The blackjack fire blazed
more fiercely red
and Cousin Billy
told us stories too sad to hear
all true

"Been on the bum"
he said soberly
"riding the rails
hard out there
Leastways I made it home
Some didn't make it back
Lordy, have mercy!

"Up there on the Great Divide
in my same boxcar
we had a nice young couple
a pretty girl
and her husband

"I remember how they
looked up at the high mountains
and down at the rushing water
then they called each other's names
locked their arms around each other
and leaped from the train"

Coda: True

My Father's Brothers

Light of foot
and heavy of hair
their witty tongues
bonded the brothers

even when they bailed
the weak one
out of jail
for being drunk
yet steady enough

to rope and hogtie
the constable
of Big Muddy

They were brothers
in failures
as well as in triumphs

They took liberties
only blood will allow
joked privately
and called each other
Blanket Indians
knowing their mother
was half Cherokee

Pies

In 1933
hope for the future
did not grow as fast
as FDR had predicted

Papa's hope for a job
did not grow at all

About all that grew
was mulberries—

back of our house
along the creek
in deepest shade

the biggest berries
I ever saw
bursting juicy dark

They made good pies
in those hard times

Some women complained
the fruit was too bland

"Add a little vinegar" Mama said
"and they will taste like blackberries
and look the same
when you cut the pie"

I remember when Papa took
his first bite of pie
he got a crinkle of hope
around his eyes

Borrowed Coats

The night was clear
as Mama's crystal cake plate
and stinging cold

Rabbits burrowed in
hollow logs
squirrels curled their
bushy tails into muffs

Toodle Barnes and I
stood at the window
of our sharecrop house
longing to go outside
and consult the moon

But our coats were much
too thin
we dared not go
though destiny called us
from the glittering sky

My younger brothers had no belief
in a magic moon—
they played dominoes by the fire
and never saw us sneak out
in their sheep-lined coats

where the moon waited
to show us its boy faces
and let us choose from them:
Toodle wavered between three faces
I looked hard and made one
irrevocable choice